ATTRACT MONEY
SUBCONSCIOUSLY: DIY

Dr Peta Stapleton

MICHELLE ANDERSON PUBLISHING

Melbourne • London

First published 2006
by Michelle Anderson Publishing Pty Ltd
P O Box 6032, Chapel Street North
South Yarra 3141 Melbourne Australia
Email: mapubl@bigpond.net.au
Website: www.michelleandersonpublishing.com

Cover design: Deb Snibson, Modern Art Production Group
Cover photograph of Author: Chris Stacey, The University of
Queensland
Typeset in Australia by Midland Typesetters, Australia
Printed in Australia by McPherson's Printing Group

National Library of Australia
cataloguing-in-publication data

Stapleton, Peta.
  Attract money subconsciously: DIY.

  Bibliography.
  ISBN 0 85572 372 6.

Self-actualization (Psychology). 2. Wealth. 3. Success.
I. Title.

158.1

Acknowledgment

My lessons in the area of money have been interesting and involved. I wish to thank my parents for providing me with the foundation to learn and the reminders of my own lessons along the way. It is always a pleasure.

Dedication

Ma and Pa: You're the best

Contents

Introduction Does Money Grow on Trees? 1

Chapter 1 What are Patterns and 7
Why Do I Have Them?

Chapter 2 Delving into Underlying 29
Beliefs

Chapter 3 The Ground-Breaking Secret 45
to Attracting Abundance

Chapter 4 Personal Growth and 49
Transformation

Chapter 5 Your Future 61

Chapter 6 Troubleshooting 79

Further Reading 87

Introduction

Does Money Grow on Trees?

Have you ever wondered why some people easily attract money into their lives and other people seem to repel it? There are a multitude of books on the market which aim to help people with their financial situation, even giving them profound hints about how to change their lives and become debt-free and healthy. These books contain fantastic information and would definitely assist some people, however they may struggle to help the people who need them the most. Let me give you an example.

$ £ €

Harry had never been that good with money. He had always earned a decent wage at the local butchery but every time he tried to save or get ahead, something happened to drain his small savings. He noticed a great book that had just been released which claimed to be able to help readers get out of the debt cycle for life and live abundantly forever! He bought the book and read it thoroughly, staying up into the wee hours of the morning to take notes. He definitely felt that this book could change his life. Harry wrote out a budget and plan for the next six months, set his short and long-term goals and committed on paper to his new strategy. Over the next few weeks he felt positive at work and referred to his plans nightly. A few weeks later he found himself doing a bit of overtime at work and forgot, or was too tired, to read his goals daily. However, he still felt optimistic; he was saving 10% of his wage and allocating money to his account for future bills. It wasn't until two months later when his car unexpectedly blew a head gasket and he immediately had to have it repaired that Harry realized his savings and bill money had to be used. He also realized that the repair bill was almost the exact amount of his savings, within $2.00! It was the story of his life and he wasn't sure what to do next.

If this story rings any bells or at least you can relate to the pattern, you will notice that even if your intention is right, if you have had a certain life pattern for as long as you can remember, then it won't respond very easily to change. The question here is: DOES MONEY GROW ON TREES? The answer is that yes, it does for some people. These people already have great patterns for easily attracting, keeping or finding money. If you would like to be one of these people, then this book is for you.

What you can expect from this book

The aim of this book is to help you identify whether you have any patterns in your life that are repelling money or preventing it from effortlessly flowing into and out of your life. Once you can identify them, you CAN change them. This book also provides a quick technique that is easily learnt and can be instantly applied to old beliefs and behaviours, and a technique for setting future goals. I do not purport to own these skills; they have existed in many forms for many years however in this book they have my flavour. I encourage you to read and explore further by accessing the books in the recommended reading section.

Once learnt, these skills can also be applied to other areas of your life where unwanted patterns may prevent other things happening. It is intended that this book be short and easy to read, however this does not undermine the science at its foundation. While these skills and techniques appear very easy and simple (they are!), should you wish to read more about the research and details governing such subconscious work, please see the following publications: Stapleton, Peta (2005) DIY: How to change subconsciously (Zeus Publications: Gold Coast).

1

What are Patterns and Why Do I Have Them?

We all have patterns in our lives. It is a reality we must face because we can then become familiar with them, and ultimately change them if we want to! Patterns can be useful and not-so-useful. Here are some examples.

Olivia had never had a problem with credibility. While she had always had a good job as a retail manager, she didn't really have any formal qualifications or training. Somehow she had just managed to work her way around the requirements and still got the job. She stood out among colleagues as a diligent and responsible employee hence her promotion to a managing position. No one ever questioned her about her lack of formal training, and when she thought about it, it had always been like that, even at school. It was just presumed that she was trustworthy, sincere and reliable. This was a pattern that worked very well for Olivia.

Janice had never been lucky in love. Every time she thought that this was the one, something invariably happened to undermine her trust and the relationship ended. Come to think of it, trust had been a big issue in Janice's life since she was left at school at age five when her mother had forgotten to come and pick her up. Janice seemed to attract issues to do with trust, even at work. While she was an honest and hard-working employee at the local library, whenever something went wrong with the computer system, she seemed to get the impression that everyone blamed her. It was uncanny and a pattern that she dearly wanted to change as it affected so many areas of her life.

So patterns can be useful or not. Here's the thing: we only want to change a pattern when it annoys us enough and we are so sick of it happening over and over again.

Patterns and money

This book is specifically about patterns in money. The first step here is to identify what patterns might be happening in your life in regards to money. Then we can discuss where they come from and how to get rid of them. If you have bought or borrowed this book from somewhere, there must be something in you that wants to shift some ideas and beliefs about money and wealth.

Our behaviours and actions are governed by our values and beliefs, and these typically come from our parents and any other significant person/institution such as schools/teachers, grandparents, close friends/neighbours. The patterns we have in our lives are in turn influenced by these values and beliefs. So let's look at some values and beliefs about wealth and abundance to see if any of them are currently hanging around in your life.

Values and beliefs about money

You only need to strike up a conversation with anyone about wealth, finances, money or abundance, and you will notice their beliefs and ideas – straight out of their mouths. How often have you heard seemingly negative comments like

- I'm just making ends meet at the moment
- Work hard. It's the only way
- There's no such thing as a free lunch/free ride
- It's hard doing it all, you know
- Things have to get worse before they get better
- You don't get something for nothing
- It's hard until it's easy
- Money always burns a hole in my pocket

- Money always slips through my fingers
- Expect the unexpected
- There's no such thing as an overnight success
- Anything worthwhile takes effort
- Money doesn't grow on trees
- Good things are worth waiting for
- Just keeping my head above water
- Scraping by
- Hanging in there
- You never get something for nothing
- I came with nothing, I'll leave with nothing
- Life's too short – live it up!
- Good things can't happen all of the time
- When things are going well, something bad has to happen
- I can never get ahead
- You must save for a rainy day

Some ideas about money itself

- It's dirty
- Filthy rich
- It's just a figure on paper

<u>And then, some seemingly positive comments</u>

- I never worry about paying bills. The money always seems to be there
- Life's a breeze, you know
- It always falls in my lap
- I always get what I want
- It's easy
- I always land on my feet

Now, be honest. Which beliefs above did you read and identify with? Jot down three to keep handy for Chapter 2.

1.

2.

3.

All of these comments are clues to underlying patterns that occur in people's lives. They might be throw-away lines at the time, but they clearly indicate beliefs. If someone continually moans that "there's no such thing as a free lunch", then it really shouldn't come as a surprise when they always have to work for everything. However, this often makes them moan louder! For one thing, they are reinforcing a belief every time they say it out loud ("there's no such thing as a free lunch"), and secondly they are continually subconsciously attracting situations in life to reinforce this belief.

Before you get despondent about these negative beliefs always hanging around, the same thing happens with positive beliefs. If you have grown up and truly believe and hence always say things like "I always get what I want", then again you always will. You probably don't think twice about it, it just happens. This may affect many areas of your life: money, jobs, relationships, sporting roles and so on.

Your beliefs about money

Some of the above examples may have hit home with you and hopefully helped the thought processes. If you find yourself getting angry, challenging some of the ideas here or feeling defensive, GOOD! I have hit the nail on the head and there are some useful things you could work with. You need to start seriously thinking about your own beliefs now about money. One of the biggest clues about your own beliefs is when you become defensive and irritated about them – especially if someone else points them out to you. You might not know why you feel so annoyed; however take it as a clue to your underlying feelings. Here is an example.

$ £ €

Victoria was constantly bombarded by those chain emails at work, asking people to sign their name and forward them on to 50 people within 2 minutes (typically to save someone's life or for a cause) otherwise something bad would happen

to her. Now, while Victoria was not overly super-
stitious and didn't really care about forwarding
them, she became really irate whenever she got
one of these emails (which was often mind you);
there was just something about them that trig-
gered anger in her. When she thought about it,
it seemed that people didn't really think about
these chain emails and forwarded them to avoid
the bad luck that might befall them if they didn't.
It was *this* stuff that really irritated Victoria –
how could people be so gullible and naïve? This
point alone upset her more than anything –
Victoria prided herself on being logical and
analytical and not accepting things at face value.
She was a thinker (her father rewarded her for
this growing up) and she was always irritated by
people who were unquestioning and uncritical.
Because this was a value in her life, and because
she *believed* (a belief!) that being critical and

analytical was a sign of higher intelligence, she was annoyed by anything which rocked this idea (eg. those chain emails). Funnily enough, she seemed to be surrounded by 'turkeys' at work who failed to be discerning and rational and she was always complaining to her husband that everyone else was an idiot! She blamed them and never quite got to the point of examining her own rigid beliefs to see if they were really serving her well.

What underlying messages reign?

On the surface, it appears that if we identify our beliefs, such as those listed, and then we let go of them or consciously try to speak differently, then our money problems (or indeed any other problems) would be solved! Sounds like a great idea, however experience suggests that money problems, debt, abundance issues and the like are tied to deeper beliefs and patterns, and they only present as financial issues on the surface. We really need to get to the bottom of what is driving them. Secondly, attempting to change them consciously will not result in permanent change. The root of all behaviour and therefore *change*, is unconscious.

Here are some suggestions of underlying beliefs.

- I'm not good enough (to have wealth, abundance, success . . .)
- I don't deserve (to have wealth . . .)
- I'm not worthy
- I'm not OK

These core beliefs will also affect other areas of your life. Here's another example.

$ £ €

Kim had always had career success. She was well-known in her area of computer technology and was regularly consulted in the print media for her opinion on the latest systems and devices. While she had always earned enough money to cover her bills, there was never really enough left over for savings or to significantly reduce existing debt. She knew she had some beliefs about money, such as *money attracts money.* Because of this belief, she never really attracted money because she didn't really have any. It was like she unconsciously avoided people who were living abundant lives, and were financially successful. Everyone in her own life always complained about debt, lack of money or some related drama, and she wasn't sure how to change it.

Through a private counselling session, Kim examined some of her own beliefs, which she knew were reinforced by her family, as her mother had always lamented about working hard, working honestly, scraping by, keeping her head over water and how tough it was "out there". Through her session Kim identified that she had some control issues about money. She handled all the money in her marriage and discovered that she *believed* that if she didn't do it herself, it wouldn't get done (eg. paying the bills, watching the debt). This didn't say much for her husband! When questioned about this, Kim said that if the bills didn't get paid, then they would be sent overdue notices and they would *get into trouble.* This was a significant revelation for Kim as she noticed in her whole life, she tried to be the good girl, and stay out of trouble. If she DID get into trouble, Kim said that it would be *all her fault* (never mind her husband) and she might be judged, misunderstood, people would get the wrong impression of her, and they might not like her!

This underlying belief was driving most of Kim's patterns and issues with money and control. When she released this, she found her worries about money subsided, it was freer to move in her life without constriction and control and money seemed to look after itself!

This example is only one but demonstrates how a deeper thought or belief often drives the outward symptoms and behaviours. There are many core beliefs and digging away at them will cause them to shift and change. Sounds good.

What's this about the subconscious?

I have just thrown in some lines about the subconscious and it is worth understanding this, as it will help you to flick those patterns – when we get to them. The subconscious mind has been described as the unconscious mind, or your inner mind. There is much written about the subconscious and the fact that it does not ever sleep – it is aware and absorbing information around you, 24 hours a day. There is even research to suggest that every second over two million pieces of information flood our aware-ness, however our conscious brain can only manage to pay attention to 7 chunks (give or take 2 chunks). (A brain absorbs 2 million bits of information per second.) Your subconscious absorbs it all. Only 7 + or – 2 chunks (or 5 to

9 chunks) are processed consciously at any one time (or 134 bits of information) – a chunk is a group of information which is manageable for you to process. So we really only process consciously, 0.000067% of all information coming in.) The subconscious though, pays attention to everything.

This explains why you remember advertisements on television (annoying, jingly, loud advertisements!), even though you don't actively sit down to memorize them. Your subconscious mind actively stores everything you have ever encountered, experienced or witnessed, from the day you were born. Even if you do not have working memories of things that happened when you were 6 months old, they are still stored within you. Some people comment that they are able to access these memories when they are deeply relaxed (eg. during meditation).

So, if you were taught certain beliefs by your parents from a young age, especially about money, and you vigorously watched your parents live out their values and principles, then it makes sense that you would absorb them and later on live them out too.

Focus

Focus is everything. What you focus upon at any given time in your life becomes your reality. Even if you don't want it to! Here is an example. Stop for a moment and try NOT to think of a red car. Do NOT think of a red car. You're not thinking of a red car are you?

The point here is that the subconscious finds it difficult to process negative information. When I suggested NOT to think of a red car, you immediately started to think about one. You might have been 'hearing' the word *don't* but because of this inability to process negatives, your subconscious started to focus upon the rest of the statement: think of a red car. It is almost as though the subconscious eliminates the word *don't* and hears the rest of the sentence, and then complies!

A perfect example here is with children. If you yell at a child "Don't run around the pool!!" they will invariably *hear* "Run around the pool" and they will. Good parenting works better if you focus on what you DO want the child to do: "Walk slowly around the pool". There is little room for misunderstanding in this sentence and no negative to eliminate. Try it!

As a third point, the subconscious does not know right from wrong. This is how you can *logically* know something (eg. you know you cannot afford the new stereo on hire purchase) but you are *emotionally* moved to do/have/be something (e.g. you buy the stereo anyway as you can always work the finances out later). This is also how the subconscious stores beliefs and memories, even though it might know something is incorrect or not useful.

$ £ €

Dan was raised with an overly critical mother. While his dad was a great provider and a family man when he wasn't working, Dan's mother was the main influence in his life. She had high standards herself and expected them from her children. Dan vividly remembers her destroying his homework sheet if he had not put enough effort into it, requesting him to start again. His mother's favourite line was "Not good enough!" and Dan took this to heart even though at a young age he did not know that he was good enough and OK! This belief which he stored popped up numerous times in his life: at work, in relationships and generally whenever he potentially could do something wrong. As an adult Dan *knew consciously* that he was good at his job and OK as a person but he could never shake the feeling that he wasn't 100% OK. His mother's throwaway line, which may not have been true, was absorbed rapidly due to its repetition and Dan believed it.

Now what?

Given we have explored some of the values and beliefs about money and abundance, it is necessary to truly uncover what is driving your patterns.

2

Delving into Underlying Beliefs

Being aware that you have some repetitive patterns in your life about money, and definitely some beliefs which would be driving them, unfortunately doesn't change them. There are several ways you can dig for and find those deeper beliefs and here are several.

Technique 1: try spending some time quietly to think about the patterns you are having in your life about money. Lie quietly with your eyes closed, preferably not when you are tired or you will fall asleep, and silently talk through the thoughts in your head. Quiet time and the dark seem to help people clarify things and reach conclusions they cannot get to when they are busy or distracted.

Technique 2: grab a pen and paper and jot down the pattern you want to change at the top. Write a question like *"Why do I have this pattern/belief* (insert the actual words here) *in my life?"*. And then put the pen in your other hand (your non-dominant hand) and let yourself answer the questions like that. You may be thinking your handwriting is terrible and you can hardly read it, but here is how it works. Very simply, research tells us that each of our brain's hemispheres controls the opposite side of our bodies. The left hemisphere controls the right side of our bodies and vice versa. People affected by stroke are testament to this. Our dominant hand draws heavily on the logical part of our opposite hemisphere because we usually use this hand to do many things in life. The suggestion is that the emotions in our brain are stored in the opposite hemisphere and so will not be readily accessed with our dominant hand. If you swap hands to write, you will be accessing the emotional component in your brain, "the inner child", as some people call it, and find out a range of things in your subconscious that perhaps you were not consciously aware of.

Technique 3: again, write down the pattern in your life you want to change. Then immediately ask yourself this question: *"How do I feel about this pattern/belief in my life?"*. Write down the FIRST thing that comes to mind, even if it doesn't make sense. It might look like this:

My Pattern – I can never get ahead in life

How I feel about this – disappointed

You might not *know* why you feel disappointed; it might have been the first feeling that came to mind. Run with it. The first step in changing a life pattern permanently is identifying its foundations. Like the example above, the underlying feeling is often nothing to do with the behaviour or pattern on the surface. The next step is to ask yourself "why". *Why* do I feel this way about xyz. If you draw a blank, push yourself – there will be something there.

Anthony had always been a conservative person. He always chose the least risky avenue, especially in work and relationships. When his first child arrived he was interested to see that his child Sam was very similar. Sam was wary of other children, avoided new situations where there might be something different (eg. a new ride in a park), and clung to his father if he was pushed to face something new. Anthony realized he was watching himself as a small child. Funnily enough, he *knew* Sam had no reason to be afraid of a new ride or new children to play with, but no amount of convincing would change Sam's ideas. It was the same with Anthony at work. If he needed to expand his customer base in his real estate job, he resisted ideas from other agents, especially if it was something radical and new. A bit like Sam, he mused.

Anthony cottoned on to some of the ideas about uncovering his feelings at a local library personal development night. He tried one of the exercises and noticed the following:

Pattern – I am scared of new things at work and risky behaviours

How I felt about this pattern – doubt my ability; low self-esteem; wanting to avoid embarrassment

These ideas gave Anthony something to work with. He had never quite thought of it in this way but was prepared to give it a go as this pattern was no longer serving his work life and certainly wasn't helping his child!

Moving towards and away: your values and beliefs

Sometimes in personal development material you read about values and beliefs and the notion of being motivated by pain or pleasure. Some people are genuinely motivated to do something *towards* a pleasurable outcome – eg. when someone puts in more time and effort at work in order to achieve that yearly holiday bonus. Other people are motivated to do something because they want to move *away* from a negative outcome – eg. a person only goes to work to earn money to AVOID getting into debt or strife with the bills.

So which one are you? Are you moving towards or away? We will get to this shortly.

You may not have thought of it like this before. However it is useful to learn your own patterns and also to learn those of significant people around you. For example, if you continually harangue your child to do their homework and threaten they will lose their special computer game for the month and it doesn't seem to have much impact upon them, perhaps they would be more motivated *towards* a more pleasurable outcome – eg. do your homework and you will be rewarded with a much desired game at the end of the month. Now some people have definite ideas about rewards and punishment with children, however I just want you to understand this concept of *towards* and *away* in relation to motivation.

Have a think about money and what it means to you in your life. Write down three things that money does for you in your life *right now* eg. money allows me to pay the bills OR money enables me to have a great holiday once a year.

1.

2.

3.

Now finish this sentence with the first thing that comes to mind: Money is important to me

....

....

The reason why I have asked you to pause to complete these exercises is to ascertain whether your ideas about money are moving you towards or away from what you want in life.

There are some big flashing lights when it comes to working out how you are motivated and they are all in your language. There tend to be three areas to watch for and these are:

1.   Negation words – don't, can't, won't
2.   Comparative words – a comparison to something else . . . so then I'll be . . .
3.   Necessity words – should, have to, must, need

If these words popped up in the sentence you completed, they may indicate that you are moving *away from* your desired state or goal. Here are some examples:

- Money is important to me because I need it to survive
- Money is important to me because you can't live without it
- I need money in my life so then I'll be comfortable

- Money is important to me because you have to pay the bills

All of these fall into one or more of the flashing light areas. They all indicate that money is a need, desperation, something you can't live without, something to struggle with, be over-whelmed by, or be powerless against. The truth is, money just is.

Go back to the three things you wrote about money and what it does for you right now in your life. These sentences will also indicate your values and ideas about money and whether you are motivated towards or away. However, there is always a flip side! Here are some examples of being motivated towards a dream or goal state:

- Money is important to me so I can help those in need

- Money is important to me so I can achieve my wildest dreams

Just keep in mind that you need to ask yourself the WHY question to work out how you are motivated. *Why is it important to have a united family? Why is it important to have a healthy diet? Why is it important to have a nest egg in the bank?*

Just say you are primarily motivated AWAY from pain or a negative state. You might say, so what? That's just the way I am! Unfortunately if you are always motivated away, you never really get what you want. You are not actually heading towards something good, just always away from something not so good. Here is how it can work with money.

Belief

I want to have more money so that I don't have to worry about paying the bills all the time.

Reality

The primary thing here that you are trying to avoid is being in a state of worrying about the bills. So even if you did get some more money (through whatever means eg. working overtime at work), and your bills were looked after and hence the worry declined, you would again eventually end up back in the state of not having enough money so the worry could return. This is because *worry is the important state for you here.* Here it is in a visual:

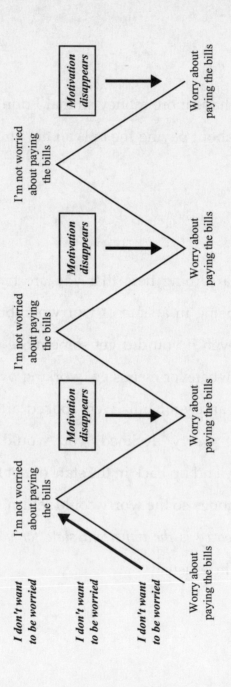

You can apply this same concept to any situation or belief you have in life where you are moving AWAY from a desired state. Remember previously we discussed the notion that the subconscious mind cannot process negatives? A mantra such as *I don't want to be broke* will never be comprehended as such. The subconscious mind will always give you what it understands – in this case, being broke!

So the first step to positive transformation in the area of money and abundance is to work out what you DO want, rather than what you DON'T want. Here is the opportunity to think about what more money and wealth will do for you and your life, in a positive way eg. more money will allow me the opportunity to study full-time and achieve my desired Arts Degree.

1.

2.

3.

Fantastic! You are on the road to re-programming that subconscious computer and achieving what you want. If you found that most of your states were moving towards a desired goal anyway, great! You are already on the right track. There must be something you still want to change though. Stay tuned for the next chapter where we will remove limiting beliefs for once and for all!

3

The Ground-Breaking
Secret to Attracting
Abundance

Your first step in attracting abundance and a new

way of thinking and being around wealth and

money, is to commit to the DECISION. It has

been said many times that the *decision* to try, do,

attempt, or endeavor to change is the very first

and necessary step. You can THINK about doing

something forever; and some people do!

However, you have reached this chapter so something is yearning for change. Yes? Let's start with a basic commitment. Here is a template for your future reference. Take the time to consider and complete it.

My Commitment to Change

Name: _____

Today is the _____ of _____, 20___. I have explored my beliefs about money and abundance and attracting wealth. And I am committed to change. I will now list my thoughts and ideas so I can review these later – and be pleasantly surprised by how much changes.

My major beliefs to change:

_____

_____

My life dreams:

_____

_____

My signature _____

47

Excellent! You have taken the first step. Go and copy the certificate and stick it somewhere prominent. And head to Chapter 4 for some skills to change your life.

4

Personal Growth and Transformation

There are a variety of techniques to work on at the subconscious level. Meditation and some spiritual work helps many people release negative events and emotions and appears to have lasting effects. However, if you want something concrete and instantly applicable, stay tuned.

Technique for overcoming past beliefs/behaviours

If you can pinpoint a belief or event that you believe has contributed to your current beliefs about money, this technique is for you. For example: you might find yourself actively saying "Money does not grow on trees" and if you *know* that your mother has also said this to you since the day you were born, then there is a probable link here. This is an event/belief you could release through this technique.

Step 1

Write down or at least think intently about the belief or event you want to release. Feel any emotions in your body and just take note of them. It is best to lie down or sit quietly at this stage and close your eyes once you have reviewed the steps.

Step 2

Imagine you can talk to yourself in your mind at this point and allow yourself to drift backwards in your past. If it is helpful, imagine there is a line in your mind that represents your life. Float backwards along the line into your earlier years. You will want to float back to the <u>very first time</u> you heard that belief or made a decision that you needed to adopt it as YOUR belief/behaviour. You need to trust your unconscious mind here in that it is taking you back to the first time, even if you cannot recall a specific memory or event. It does not matter if you recall anything. You are just going on a gut feeling. The point is that you cannot do any harm.

Step 3

When you instinctively or intuitively know you have reached the point in your past, pause there and notice if any feelings pop up. You might just feel certain emotions or notice sensations in your body. Just let the thoughts float in and let them go. You need to really start thinking at this point. It is time to let your cognitive mind work!

There will always be positive or good reasons why you took on such a belief or made decisions about money and abundance. For example:

$ £ €

Kay had a belief that she could only earn good money by working hard and long hours. She wanted to remove this belief to open up other opportunities in her life. She got to this part in the exercise and discovered that such a belief helped her feel committed and worthwhile. She realized that by working hard and long hours, she avoided anyone thinking she was lazy or taking shortcuts. And this belief helped her feel good. This is why the belief and behaviour was useful for many years.

Step 4

Still with your eyes closed, imagine all the positive learnings and good reasons stacking up and being stored in some type of container next to you in your mind. You need to keep all the good parts in that container. If you CANNOT think of one good reason, just ask your unconscious mind to find you something to store, and imagine that it does this for you. It does not matter if you CONSCIOUSLY think of anything; it will still happen at the subconscious level.

It is time to let go of the negative feelings and belief now. Imagine you can see the belief or decision way beneath you represented as a dot, and imagine the negatives associated with it hang from your body. It is almost as though you have moved back a little further in time where you are looking at that belief dot in front of you from a point BEFORE you ever made it. You can now let the belief/behaviour go; imagine they drop away from your body, they flick off, they fall below and leave you free. As this happens, imagine you can now make a new decision or belief to replace the old one. It might be the opposite of the old one (eg. Kay's new belief was "I am free to earn abundant income in my normal work hours"), or you might just get a new idea. Imagine the new belief or decision is a colour and this floods your body now; filling you inside and out. Imagine you can float forward into your future and back to today.

As you float along, you might notice the colour spreading around, heading up towards the future and brightening things.

Is it that easy?

Sometimes people want things to be difficult. Because of our conditioning we might think over-coming our beliefs or behaviours needs to be long and difficult. The reality is that this is just a belief!! Your subconscious will do anything you request, as long as you ask correctly, or adopt the right belief in the first place. So the answer is, yes it is this easy.

I like the onion analogy, often used to explain how we have layers of beliefs and behaviours. Like an onion, if you discard an old belief or behaviour and then you notice something else in its place, it may be that the underlying belief would not have presented itself until you removed the outer layer. Core beliefs (at the centre of the onion) are the important ones to get to, and these were the ones we were alluding to in Chapter 1. The more of these core beliefs (eg. I am not worthy) that you can discard, the more changes will happen in many areas of your life.

A script for "letting go" technique

Below is a script for the above technique. You may find it easy to hand someone else this script and just ask him or her to read it to you <u>word for word</u>, until you remember the technique on your own. Ask them to read it slowly.

Sit back and relax and close your eyes. Begin to focus on your breathing; noticing that breath as you breathe in and breathe out. (Pause). Begin to think about the belief or behaviour (insert actual words if you know them) you are wanting to change. Notice any feelings that might be in your body when you think of this belief. (Pause). When you are ready, begin to drift backwards into your past and if it is helpful, notice a line which extends into the past. Float along that line. It represents your life. Ask your subconscious mind to take you back to the very first time you made the decision to adopt that belief or behaviour. Keep floating and stop when you feel it is the right point. (Pause).

Do not be concerned if you do not remember a memory. Trust that your subconscious will guide you back to the first time.

Just imagine the first time is a dot on your line. It is way beneath you and seems really tiny. Just hover over it now and notice any feelings that might be present. Take note of these. (Pause).

It is time now to store all of the positive reasons and intentions associated with this belief/behaviour. Imagine there is a container or vessel next to you in your mind where you can store all of the good reasons you adopted this belief/behaviour. Be your own best cheerleader or coach and ask your subconscious mind to start to store all of the good reasons you took on this belief/behaviour and made it your own. (Pause). Trust that this process is happening, even if you cannot consciously think of any positive reasons. Your subconscious mind is still at work. (Pause). Know that all the good and helpful reasons you adopted that old belief will stay with you always, ready to be drawn upon when you need them. (Pause).

Imagine you can now make a decision to let go of

the old belief/behaviour. Imagine you are still looking at it as a tiny dot below you. You are almost looking at it in front of you but way beneath. It is as though you have moved back in time even further to a time when you hadn't made that decision. It is in front of you. (Pause). Now it is time to let go. You might see it as a weight falling away from your body. You might feel it drop away and leave you. Ask your subconscious mind to let go of the decision made all those years ago. And as this happens, imagine a colour floods your body and fills you completely. (Pause).

As you experience that colour and start to move forward into your future, that colour spreads around you and streams ahead. Your mind starts to prepare for a new decision. As you hover above that point which you know is today, imagine you get to make a new decision and belief. It might be the direct opposite of the old belief; it might be a new word which springs to mind right now. (Pause). Store that positive belief now and look towards the future, noticing how bright and clear it seems. Enjoy this moment. (Pause).

When you are ready, start to focus upon your breathing and notice how your body is resting. Gradually allow yourself to come back into the room and when you are ready, gently open your eyes.

5

Your Future

Some of the most exciting work in this field is the work with subconscious goal setting or future pacing. It stands to reason that if you can discard old beliefs and replace them with new ones, you can certainly move ahead into the future and create a whole new life for yourself – and your subconscious mind will see that it happens. Remember that the subconscious mind does not understand TIME (which is why some people who experience a traumatic breakup 12 years ago can still be reliving it today as though it had just happened). The subconscious does not understand time in the past – and it does not understand time in the future. You can literally reprogram your future mind to achieve anything you want!

There is a humorous statement which says: Some people make things happen, some watch things happen, and some wonder what happened.

This brings us to the notion of setting goals in life. A lack of a firm objective is the number one reason for that feeling of uncertainty in life – humans appear to need goals. Regardless of whether we set specific goals or even large ones, we all have plans we follow. Waking up each morning is a goal! Recently an employee I knew of was submitting all of his holidays for the year in advance. When asked why he was applying for his holidays a whole year in advance, he replied, "So I have something to look forward to."

An almost magical way to help you achieve your goals is by using your subconscious. Seeing your goals in your "mind's eye" is like planting them in your subconscious – and success is assured!

$ £ €

Kass was a successful hairdresser and had a great following of regular clients in a local salon. She made the decision to cease working for someone else and set out to create her own mobile hairdressing service. She intended to visit clients in the comfort of their own homes and provide the same service they would get in a salon. With this decision came a bunch of feelings about making enough money. Kass was a little anxious about the number of clients she needed to see per week in order to generate the same, if not better, income as she had had in a job. It didn't matter if there was a cancellation in the salon as she still got paid, but a cancellation or lack of bookings in her own business was a different matter. Kass applied some of the future pacing techniques on a weekly basis and lo and behold, she was booked up in a short space of time and didn't give her income a second thought. She consciously made a decision at the beginning of each week as to how many clients she wanted to service and the income she wanted to earn, and the rest fell into place with the future goal setting technique.

The rules

There are rules with goal setting in order to give your subconscious mind the best possible chance of succeeding. The first is **make sure the goal is something you WANT**. Remember the chapter where we explored whether you are motivated towards or away from things; this is the time to recall your natural orientation. Sometimes people set goals because they feel they have to, or it is necessary and it is not really something they want.

The second point is to set goals using a common acronym (SMART) to demonstrate what I mean. When setting goals you need to make sure your goal fits these areas.

S – Specific (it needs to be VERY specific)
M– Measurable (how will you KNOW when

you have achieved it? You need to measure the outcome in some way)

A– Attainable (this means for YOU. Can you actually achieve such a goal?)

R – Realistic (is it a genuine goal for YOU?)

T – Time framed (you need an end point of WHEN you know it will be achieved)

I would throw in at this point that your goal should be positive and not harmful to yourself, others or the environment.

Here is an example of an excellent goal.

<u>**Goal**</u> – to achieve a weight loss of 5 kilograms by December 15th, 2006; by jogging or walking for 30 minutes every Monday, Wednesday and Friday afternoon.

S – it is specific. I am not just saying I am going to lose weight. I am going to lose

5 kilograms and I have stated HOW I am going to do this

M– it is measurable as I will be able to see on the scales how much I have lost

A – it is attainable for me

R – it is realistic for me

T – it is time framed as I have an end-goal (a specific date) to reach

It would be unrealistic for me to set a goal to win the tennis at Wimbledon. I am absolutely uncoordinated with a tennis racket and am not even an amateur player, let alone someone with a ranking. When you get into this technique and realize its potential in your life, it might be attractive to start planting some money/abundance goals in your future. You never know what will happen.

Remember that your future goals fit with your current beliefs and behaviours. If you want to win lotto and buy tickets every week and fail to ever get 3 numbers, you need to ask yourself about your motive and past patterns of winning. If you have never won a raffle in your life, winning lotto might not fit with your current beliefs about winning or deserving to get something for free (ah-hah! A belief maybe!). However, if your motive to win lotto is driven by a want to stay at home to be a full-time parent but still have an income, then maybe there are other options out there to fulfill this besides winning lotto. When you cotton onto the REAL reason for wanting something, your subconscious will help you.

Technique for future goal setting

Step 1: Focus on the End-Point. Either write about or imagine the very moment you will know you have achieved/arrived at the goal you desire. This is the MOST important part. You need to be very specific and pick a date. Now if you do not really know a date (eg. you want to buy a house in the next 12 months but you don't know exactly when), pick a date that seems reasonable and attainable to you. Any date will do. Add a year too! Use this formula when setting any future goals:

It is now_____20____

(insert actual day, month, year)

And I am _____

_____

(complete the description here)

Here are some examples.

It is now March 18th, 2006 and I am standing on the verandah of my home, holding the mortgage papers to my home. I have just paid the final installment on my loan and I now own my own home. I feel fantastic.

It is now December 24th, 2008 and I am sipping hot chocolate in my holiday chalet in the Swiss Alps, preparing to wrap the Christmas presents for my three children. It is snowing outside.

Step 2: Read this step first or alternatively get someone to read the script to you. Close your eyes and imagine you are IN the actual picture of that end-goal. It is happening around you. You are experiencing the end-point of that goal, as though it is happening right now. Imagine the feelings you are feeling, the sensations in your body, the wonderful thoughts in your mind. Make the picture as bright, vivid or intense as you like.

Step 3: Now step out of the picture and imagine you are holding the image as a photograph in your hand. You are no longer in the picture but you are looking at yourself in the photograph, in the snapshot moment. You need to also imagine the line in your mind now which represents your future. It will shoot off into the future. Imagine you can float along that line into the future to that EXACT date you set. You will instinctively know when you are floating above it.

Step 4: Now drop that photo down into the line so it takes its place in the future, exactly where you say it will happen. Notice how things might change around you while you are looking at the line; everything is moving to support you achieving that goal. Float back to today and return to the room. Open your eyes.

A script – "end-goal" visualization technique

This technique is designed to be short and quick, and can be done on a daily basis if you want.

Close your eyes and imagine you are IN the actual picture of that end-goal you desire. It is happening all around you. You are experiencing the end-point of that goal, as though it is happening right now. Imagine the feelings you are feeling, the sensations in your body, the wonderful thoughts in your mind. Make the picture as bright, vivid or intense as you like. (Pause). Now step out of the picture and imagine you are holding the image as a photograph in your hand. You are no longer in the picture but you are looking at yourself in the photograph, in the snapshot moment. Now imagine the line in your mind that represents your future. It will shoot off into the future that is yet to happen. (Pause). Imagine you can float along that line into the future to that EXACT date you set for your goal. You will instinctively know when you are floating above it. (Pause). In a moment you will drop that photo down into the line. Not yet. Just hover above the date for a moment. (Pause). Now drop that photo down into the line so it takes its place in the future, exactly where you say it will happen. Notice how things might change around you while you are looking at the line; everything is moving to support you achieving that goal. Float back to today and return to the room. Open your eyes.

The important things in this exercise include:

1. Associating with the picture first and seeing yourself in it now
2. Stepping out of the picture so you are holding it as a photograph

This ensures that your subconscious mind does not think you have already achieved it and not set into motion the things which need to happen for it to be fulfilled. Have you ever met anyone who acts as though they are far superior at work, of a certain standing in society or someone they are not, and it is clear they are none of these things? Sometimes people naturally do the future goal setting exercise in their everyday lives and imagine what it is they want or who they want to be, however they fail to step out of the picture and place it in the future as a magnet. Which means they fail to move towards it and make it authentic. They are essentially deluding themselves that it has already happened and that they do not need to do anything to get there.

$ £ €

Freya worked as a national distributor for a pharmaceutical company. She was very good at her work and prided herself on her ability to relate well to a range of people. She consistently ranked in the top 5 people of the company but itched to be number one. She worked out how many customers she needed to sell to on a weekly basis in order to reach the monthly target. She set the end-goal: It is January 31st, 2006 and I am looking at the monthly tally sheet in the head office, and my name is number one for the month December. She completed the future goal exercise with this in mind. However, in the month of December, at the start of each day, she also sat in her car before she entered work for the day and set the goal. It may have been a certain number of telephone calls she needed to make with a certain number of positive responses, or it may have been a quantity of stock she needed to sell. Whatever the daily goal, she set it every day and always imagined herself at the end of that day, feeling relaxed and enthused by her day's work. It never failed to deliver.

Where to from here?

The world is literally in your hands. We have focused on the power of the subconscious mind in order to let go of limited beliefs, old decisions and behaviours in the area of wealth, abundance and solid financial success and in addition have touched upon ways to create future success. You may have noticed by now that problems to do with the flow of money in your life may not necessarily be about money. Issues of self-esteem, love, confidence or sense of worth may be at the foundations, and overcoming these will free issues of abundance at the same time.

I enjoy hearing from readers and welcome the opportunity to include your personal stories of success and accomplishment in future books. Please feel free to contact me:

Dr Peta Stapleton

P.O. Box 1060

MUDGEERABA, QUEENSLAND,

AUSTRALIA 4213

www.petastapleton.com

Wishing you enormous success and prosperity!

6

Troubleshooting

This chapter has been included for any questions which may come to mind.

What if I fall asleep during any of the processes?

If a therapist is helping you with these techniques and they are talking to you while you fall asleep, it does not seem to make a difference.

Therapists can use signals (like asking you to raise one finger when you are ready to move on during the process) and people appear to continue doing this even when they fall asleep.

However, if you are doing the techniques by yourself and fall asleep, the process seems to stop. You must try again at another time when you are not tired. Keep in mind that the subconscious is strong and you may start to feel sleepy during a technique, even if you did not beforehand! The subconscious may be trying to divert you from changing a pattern that has been useful for you until this point.

How do I know if the technique has worked?

The best way to check this is to get back out there and see if the pattern/belief happens again. Because these techniques are subtle yet powerful, you may have to pay particular attention to the area in life you wanted to change. What seems to happen is that the behaviour changes and things just start to work out and it is a while before you realise it used to be different! This is because the new behaviour seems so normal!

Do I have to believe in these techniques for them to work?

Sometimes people think they need to believe in techniques like these for them to work however, this is not the case when working with the subconscious. As long as you follow the process (or have someone do it for you), your behaviour and patterns will change. Of course, if you do not believe in it and do not give it a go, nothing will change!

I have done the exercise but the pattern still seems to persist!

There is a chance that you have not got to the bottom of the pattern if this happens. Sometimes our patterns are very intricate and while you will definitely change some aspect of it during a process, the part you might really want to change may be buried a bit deeper. I liken it to an onion. If you peel back one layer of the onion, it then allows you to peel back the next layer, and so on. It can be the same with patterns. Unless you do a first technique, you might not be able to become aware of the next thing you need to change. Patterns will change

along the way until finally the core or foundation of the pattern changes. There is no set
number of techniques you need to do before
this happens. It is all individual. The good news
is, you will hit some of the patterns on the head
first time around!

So, if I do not believe in these techniques and do not do them, is there any other way (or any other techniques) that will change my patterns?

I am not aware of any other techniques, which
will so easily change patterns on a subconscious
level. Many therapists teach clients techniques
which target the conscious mind (like learning
appropriate thoughts) but they take a lot of

conscious effort. There may be other subconscious techniques out there; this is just one that has worked very easily.

What if I cannot work out what I want to change?

This one is over to you. Spend some time thinking about different areas in your life and decide what you are unhappy about. You may find it is a physical sensation that you do not like, for example a pounding heart or wavering voice when you speak in public. If you are still stuck, ask someone in your life what they do not like about your behaviour! This will give you food for thought.

What if I cannot relax enough to do a technique?

You really do not need to be completely relaxed in order for these techniques to work. For first timers, it is often useful to relax and lie down in order to fully access the subconscious and learn. Once you are used to the techniques, you can do them quickly and anywhere! I have worked with some clients who do not need to close their eyes!

When can I stop doing the techniques?

You can stop at any time. However, you will usually become aware of something else you want to change down the track. It is the onion analogy again. Peeling back layers will make you aware of other patterns buried more deeply. The time in between techniques will vary – you may do several a day and then nothing for months. It is up to you.

What if I find it difficult to focus during the technique (and I start daydreaming about other stuff)?

This can happen to us all. You can either try again at another time or persevere until you stay focused. If you find this is a general pattern in your life anyway (ie. you always have difficulty focusing and everyone tells you so), you could always work on that theme first!! If you change that behaviour, other things will change in your life.

Reference: Stapleton, Peta (2005). DIY: How to change subconsciously. Zeus Publications: Gold Coast.

Further Reading

Ageless Body, Timeless Mind by Deepak Chopra,
M.D. – Ageless Body: Timeless Mind, Deepak
Chopra, 1994, Harmony: USA

Awaken the Giant Within by Anthony Robbins –
1992, Free Press, USA

Creating Affluence: Wealth Consciousness in the
Field of All Possibilities by Deepak Chopra,
M.D. – 2002, Excel Books

Frogs Into Princes by Richard Bandler & John Grinder – 1979, Real People Pr

Perfect Health: The Complete Mind/Body Guide by Deepak Chopra, M.D. –

Perfect Health: The Complete Mind/Body Guide, Deepak Chopra, 2001, Harmony: USA

Quantum Healing by Deepak Chopra, M.D. – 1990, Bantam

Rich Dad, Poor Dad by Robert Kiyosaki – 1997, TechPress, Arizona, USA

10 Secrets for Success and Inner Peace. Dr Wayne Dwyer – 2002, Hay House, USA

The Dynamic Laws of Prosperity by Catherine Ponder – 1985, DeVorss & Company

The Journey by Brandon Bays – The Journey, Brandon Bays, 1999, Thorsons: London

Turning Passions into Profits: Three Steps to Wealth and Power by Christopher Howard – 2004, Wiley & Sons, New Jersey, USA

You can Heal Your Life by Louise Hay – Hay House, California USA, 2004